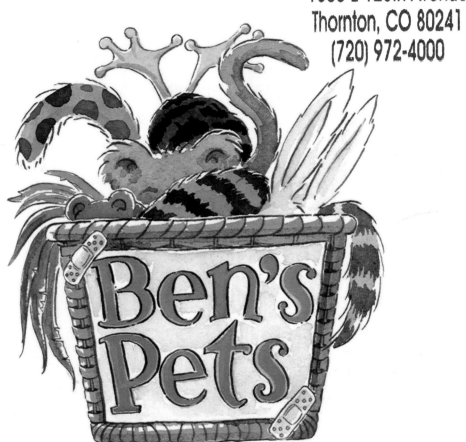

Ben's Pets

Written by Anne Miranda
Illustrated by Michael Chesworth

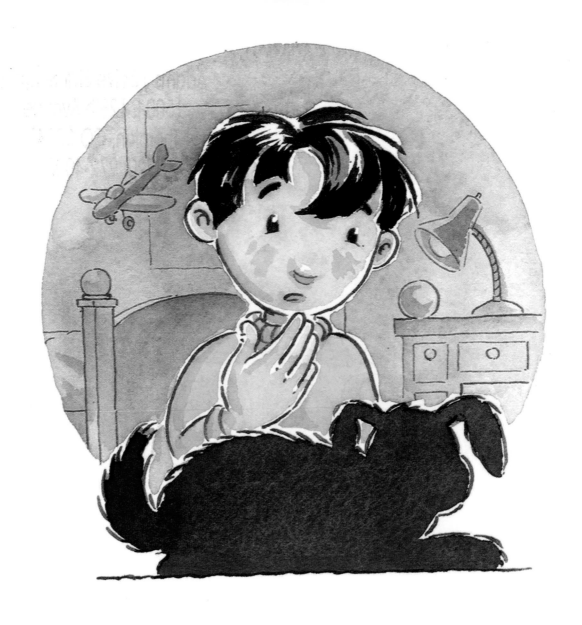

My pet dog is sick.

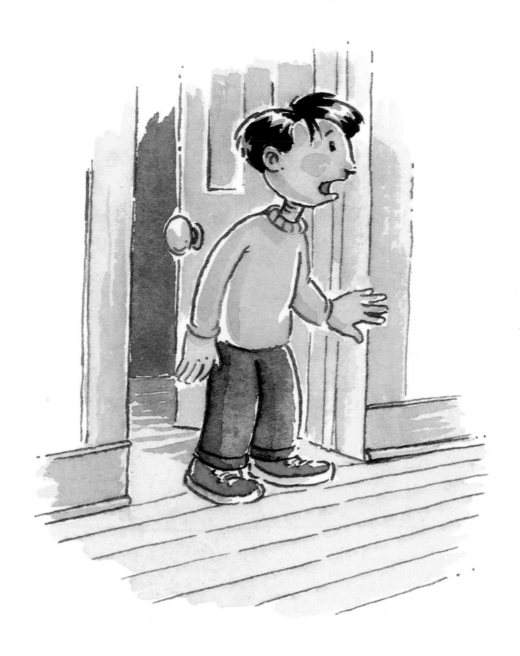

Get the vet.

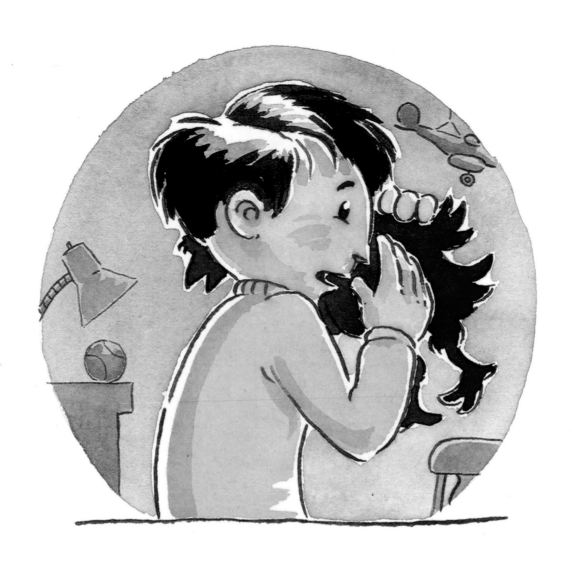

My pet hen is sick.

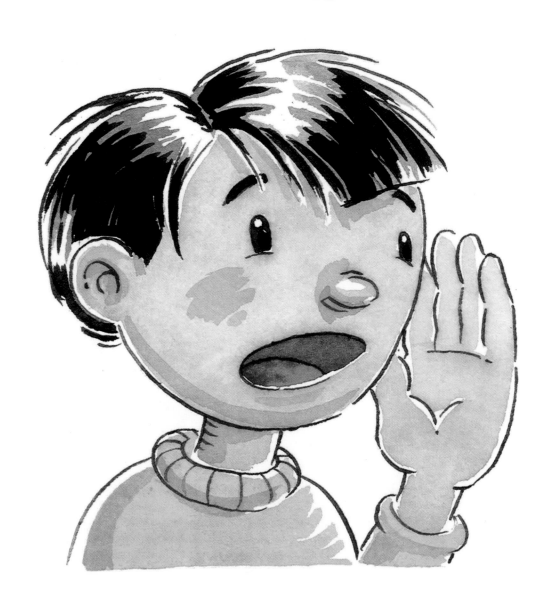

Get the vet!

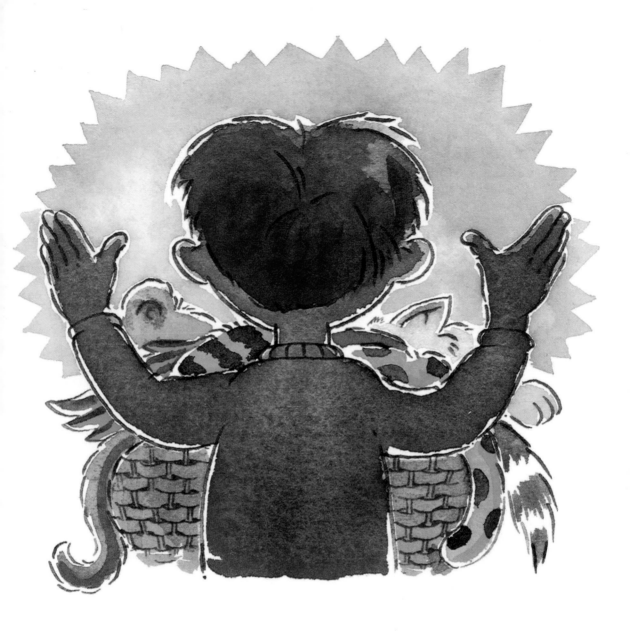

All my pets are sick.
GET THE VET!

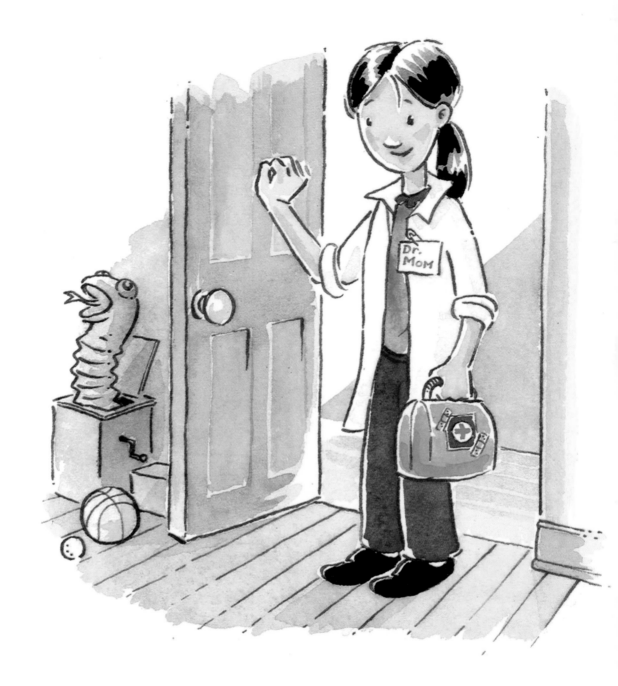

The vet is here.

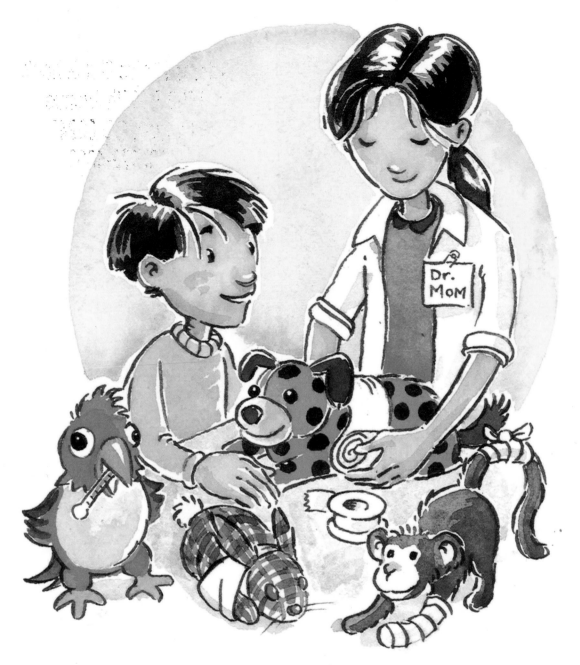

Thanks, Mom.